5. Designate a staff person to ⟨...⟩ nesses.
6. Preserve crime scene (for tho⟨...⟩ is not known and/or serious injury has occurred).
7. Call the police/security.
8. Notify parents of involved students.
9. Assign a staff person to remain with the victim while medical attention is being obtained.
10. Assign a staff person to remain with assailant until police/security or the administrator who is going to conduct an investigation arrives on the scene.

Special Note

More teachers and administrators are injured while breaking up fights and assaults than during any other type of activity. This occurs because the person breaking up the altercation makes several critical mistakes.

First, the adult runs up to the fight and immediately jumps into the middle of the fracas and starts pulling the combatants apart. This action offers the kids a free shot at the adult. After all, in the heat of the fight how could they possibly know that it was a teacher pulling them apart? They thought it was some other student!

The second critical mistake adults make is that they do not take the time to analyze the fight. By jumping right into the middle of the dispute, the adult does not know if one or both of the fighters has a weapon or if the altercation is a staged event, staged for the benefit of the teacher or administrator; or if the fight is in the winding down stage, meaning both kids are pooped; or who the aggressor is. You want to know who has, or is getting the better blows in, because that's the person you must watch.

The recommended procedure for breaking up altercations involves the following steps:

- *Walk*, don't run to the fight.
- The moment you come in sight of the altercation use your best cafeteria voice and let the world know you are coming and you want this nonsense stopped immediately.
- If possible, while *walking* to the fight, stop at various classrooms and obtain help from other teachers; make sure someone is sent to the office for additional help.

- Call out to any of the students you recognize and start giving orders: Mary, go to Mr. Frank's room; Sam, you go to the office and get Mr. Jones; Calvin, go to your locker and get me your science book. It doesn't matter what you tell the kids to do. Just remember, kids are accustomed to responding to directions, so give them directions. You want them away from the commotion.
- If you know the fighters by name, call out each of their names and let them know you know who they are. This may be the time for a little humor. If you can get some of the kids laughing, it will ease the tension.
- If you are confronted with a real donnybrook of a fight, get additional help. Don't try to be a hero.

INVESTIGATIVE TECHNIQUES

A. For cases that are going to be handled administratively, i.e., not referred to police/security for prosecution:

1. Have the parties involved prepare a written statement about the events as they perceive them.
2. Have each witness prepare a written statement.
3. Allow a cooling off period before attempting to bring the parties together. The length of time needed for the cooling off period will vary from incident to incident.
4. Ascertain the causes of the dispute. Very often a third party will have been the instigator of the altercation and it is important to identify this person and treat him/her as an active participant in the incident.
5. Follow established procedures with regard to suspension or detention.
6. Solicit from each of the participants a written agreement regarding future behavior.
7. Determine where the students should have been at the time of the assault/fight.
8. Prepare a written report of the entire incident, including the time first notification was made of the assault/fight and the chronological order of events, listing the names and times notifications were made. Investigative

reports should include a statement of the intent of the parents of the victim as to the course of action they are considering, i.e., filing criminal charges, filing civil suit for recovery of damages.

9. In cases involving the allegation that a staff person assaulted a student, it is recommended that the superintendent be notified as well as the attorney for the board of education.

10. Analyze the incident to ascertain what steps, if any, could have been taken to prevent this incident.

B. For cases in which criminal prosecution is anticipated:

1. Isolate all witness(es), assailant(s), and victim(s) pending the arrival of police/security.

2. If a weapon is involved, maintain custody of the weapon until it is turned over to the police/security. Obtain a written receipt for the weapon.

3. Notify parents of students involved.

4. Assign a staff person to remain with victim until police/security arrive.

5. If victim is transported to a medical facility, have a staff person accompany victim.

6. Prepare a written narrative of the event including the names and times all persons were notified of the event.

7. If the assailant is not known, it is imperative that the scene of the assault/fight be secured until the police/security can conduct a crime scene search. This may require assigning several staff members to the area and not allowing anyone other than the police/security to enter the area.

8. Be prepared to answer inquiries from the news media. If the case is going to be handled by the police/security, coordinate any press releases with the officer on the scene.

OTHER CONSIDERATIONS

1. Extent of injury—Each assault/fight report should include a statement as to the extent of injury. The following classifications are recommended:

a. no medical attention required
b. first aid required (administered by school personnel)
c. medical attention required (provided by a physician).

2. Determine whether or not the assault/fight will have additional ramifications for the school and/or the community. It may be advisable to request that additional personnel be assigned to the school for a short period of time to help reduce levels of anxiety or fear on the part of students and staff. Police should be advised if it appears that the incident will spread to the community.

3. For serious assaults/fights it is advisable to discuss the incident with the faculty and perhaps representatives of the student body. It is important to have the actual facts disseminated rather than to allow rumors to sread.

4. At some point a parent/student conference will have to be held. This conference should not take palce until there are assurances that the parties involved can discuss the issues without escalating the animosity between the students.

5. If the origin of the dispute is a community/neighborhood conflict, it may be advisable to involve neutral community leaders, i.e., clergy, juvenile service personnel, recreation leaders, etc. in the conference. All parties should agree to involvement of outsiders prior to the conference.

Bomb Incidents

Bomb: Any device containing combustible material and a fuse.

Subcategories:
1. a. threat
   b. device found
   c. explosion
2. (1) no injury
   (2) personal injury
   (3) property damage
   (4) both personal injury and property damage

PREVENTION STRATEGIES

In a realistic sense, a school administrator can do little to prevent a bomb incident. Unlimited access to telephones, an endless list of explosive and incendiary materials, and access to "underground" publications, which offer handy tips to the would-be bomber, make "prevention" something less than an exact science. Some general strategies can be employed, but they are limited.

1. Require that all chemical storage areas be locked and that careful inventory be maintained on those chemicals that can be used to make explosive compounds.
2. All of the Target Hardening Techniques[1] discussed for the protection of buildings are applicable, in the sense that a secure building makes illegal entry more difficult.
3. Establish written procedures with staff who answer telephones on how to handle a "bomb threat."
4. Be watchful for publications that furnish instructions for making bombs. *The Anarchist Cookbook, School Stoppers Handbook, Underground Manual Number 3* are several that have made the rounds of schools.
5. Never lose track of the fact that a bomb threat and the placement of a bomb in a school is a form of terrorism. It should never be viewed as a prank or some childish act.

RESPONSE PROCEDURES

A. **Bomb threat**
1. Call the police.
2. Evaluate the threat. On the basis of evidence, experience, and judgment, is the threat credible?
    (a) evidence:
        —sign of illegal entry into the school
        —report of missing chemicals
        —no sign of illegal entry.
    (b) experience:
        —all other bomb threats have proven to be a hoax
        —tests are scheduled for today

---

[1] Target Hardening Techniques are discussed in detail beginning on Page 22.

—today is the first warm day of Spring
—today is Senior Skip Day
—your school is playing its rival school in an athletic event
—the caller was obviously a youngster and there was giggling in the background when the call was received
—unexplained student unrest
—employee strike.

judgment:
—based on all the available information the threat is or is not credible.

3. Conduct a limited search of the building.
4. Consult with the police on the scene.

B. **Device found**

1. Call the police.
2. Isolate the area.
3. Evacuate the school by stages (don't pull the fire alarm as this may require students and staff to walk directly near the device—evacuate by room, starting with those rooms nearest the device).
4. *Do not handle the suspected device—leave that to the experts.*
5. Reenter the building only after being advised to do so by the officer in charge.

C. **Explosion**

1. Assuming for the moment that the person-in-charge didn't cease to exist as the result of the explosion, and the phones still work, all of the following suggestions are applicable:
   (a) Call the police and fire departments
   (b) Evacuate the remainder of the building
   (c) Develop a list of casualties
   (d) Refer to page xv (Emergency Telephone Numbers) and call your lawyer. This is particularly important in those cases in which a bomb threat had been received and you made the decision not to evacuate the school.

2. Pending arrival of emergency equipment and additional help, get the students and staff to a safe location and maintain control of the students.

3. Whether or not the building will be reoccupied will be a decision made by the fire department and/or the police department. In either case, the following steps will need to be followed:

   (a) Notify the superintendent

   (b) Establish an information center staffed by senior officials who will be able to handle all inquiries about injured persons and the status of the school.

   (c) Arrange transportation for the students, should the school be closed.

INVESTIGATIVE TECHNIQUES

All bomb incidents need to be handled by individuals who are specially trained in these matters. Be guided by their recommendations and offer whatever assistance you can to identify possible suspects.

Burglary

Burglary: The unlawful removing, taking or carrying away of property from a school building that is legally closed.

Note: The last employee has left the school and the school has been secured.

Subcategories:

1. a. actual
   b. attempted
2. (1) property theft under $100
   (2) property theft over $100
   (3) property damage under $100
   (4) property damage over $100
   (5) combined property theft and damage under $100
   (6) combined property theft and damage over $100

PREVENTION STRATEGIES

The key to prevention of property loss rests with the school's ability to implement and maintain "target hardening techniques." Target hardening is the process by which physical protective devices, internal management controls, and the careful deployment of security personnel are combined and coordinated in such a manner as to make the objectives of the criminal more difficult to achieve.

Target hardening always has an important judgmental factor. What *resources* will be needed to reduce what *risks* to what *desired level of acceptability?* Target hardening has these general objectives:

1. To prevent the crime from occurring.
2. To make the criminal's task so difficult as to make his/her objective less desirable.
3. To slow the criminal down, thus increasing his/her chances of being apprehended.
4. To give warning of illegal entry.
5. To remove objects of value from sight.
6. To develop a security awareness on the part of administrators, teachers, custodians, students, and other staff members.

A number of strategies can be used to meet the objectives of target hardening techniques.

A. Building:
   1. Inspect all exterior door locks to ensure they are in good working condition.
   2. Install a burglar alarm system, giving special care to cover the following areas:
      (a) classrooms and offices containing office equipment
      (b) musical instrument storage areas
      (c) food storage areas
      (d) stairwells—if multiple storied building
      (e) intersection of hallways
      (f) area where student records are maintained
      (g) areas where athletic equipment is stored
      (h) areas where chemicals are stored

(i) principal's office (the principal may not keep anything of value in the office, but it is nice to protect the boss's possessions, regardless of value).
3. Have broken windows repaired as quickly as possible.
4. *Limit, limit, limit* distribution of keys. When keys are issued have each recipient sign for the key received. Periodically check to see that employees have their assigned keys.
5. If school is two or more stories, try to place business education classes on an upper floor.
6. *Keep storage rooms locked at all times.*
7. Remove all signs that identify what is behind a closed door. (There is no reason to advertise that a certain room is used for storage of audiovisual equipment.)

B. Contents:
1. Require, demand, insist upon frequent inventory of all serialized equipment.
2. Require, demand, insist that all inventories be signed and dated by the person(s) conducting the inventory (this becomes particularly important in the event property is stolen and the police want to know the last time the object was seen).
3. Implement a "sign-out" log for all audiovisual equipment normally stored in an area other than the classroom.
4. When equipment is sent out for repair, require a signed receipt from the person picking up the equipment.
5. Inspect contents of all delivered equipment and supplies (don't just count boxes, look inside; once delivery has been signed for, the carrier is off the hook if the equipment is not in the box).
6. Require, demand, insist that all school equipment have the school name inscribed some place on the equipment (it may not look very pretty, but having the school name painted in a bright color sure cuts down on the marketability of that item).
7. Require, demand, insist that small pieces of equipment, such as tape recorders, phonographs, pocket cal-

culators, balance beam scales, etc., are locked up each day and not left sitting on a ground floor window sill.

8. If the borrowing of school property is permitted (heaven forbid), require a signed receipt for the property and hold the borrower *liable* if the property is lost, stolen or damaged while in his/her custody.

9. Do not keep large amounts of money in school overnight (anything under $50 is usually okay).

10. *All administrators*—empty your bottom right/left hand desk drawer of all confiscated property, i.e., drugs, booze, girly magazines, porno flicks, guns, knives, clubs, etc. (There are documented cases where schools were burglarized just so the culprit could get to the bottom desk drawer of school administrators who confiscate materials found on the school grounds.)

C. General:

1. Require, demand, insist, that all suspected property losses be reported immediately (don't let days or weeks go by under the guise that the responsible person was "looking" for the missing property).

2. Make property protection a high priority by discussing property protection procedures at staff meetings and at parent meetings. (Let the community know that your school has taken "undisclosed" steps to protect its property and that any unauthorized person found with school property will be prosecuted.)

3. Meet with police department officials and solicit their help, support, and suggestions for improving your school's security. (Every police department has a Crime Prevention Unit; they will be more than happy to assist in any way they can to help you protect your school.)

RESPONSE PROCEDURES

1. Call the police upon discovery of a burglary.

2. Protect the crime scene until the police arrive (keep all persons away from the immediate area until the police have had an opportunity to examine the area).

3. Conduct an immediate inventory and prepare a list of all missing equipment, making sure you have the manufacturer's name, serial number, model number, color, value, and all other identifying characteristics of the stolen equipment (all of this information will be available from the inventory report).

INVESTIGATIVE TECHNIQUES

1. Attempt to determine if the property stolen has any resale value (this will provide a clue as to who the thief might be).
2. Determine who the last person was who (a) saw the missing property and (b) secured the area from which the property was taken.
3. Review past incidents. What happened in the past few days that might have led to this burglary? A disgruntled student, employee, or parent, unrest in the school, employee strike, community unrest, dissatisfaction with the principal's leadership abilities, someone who has shown an interest in the item(s) stolen, etc.
4. Consider offering a reward for information leading to the recovery of the property. (Note: your primary concern should be in the recovery of the property, not in identifying who committed the offense.)
5. Make sure that the stolen property was taken as the result of the burglary and was not taken during school hours (a larceny) with the appearance of a burglary being used to cover up an employee theft.

Drugs/Narcotics/Alcohol

Drug/Narcotic: Any illegal substance, including alcohol, which when taken internally or smoked, causes a change in a person's behavior.

Subcategories:

1. a. use
   b. possession

c.　sale/distribution
　　d.　overdose
　　e.　found
　　f.　suspicion
　2.　(1)　marijuana
　　　(2)　amphetamines
　　　(3)　barbiturates
　　　(4)　hallucinogens
　　　(5)　beer
　　　(6)　wine
　　　(7)　liquor
　　　(8)　other
　　　(9)　unknown

PREVENTION STRATEGIES

No other offense has the potential for causing as many problems for a school as do drugs. Not only must administrators deal with not only administratively, but in each and every case in which aware of the other related offenses that are often associated with drugs on a school campus. No one knows the number of fights, robberies, larcenies/thefts, weapons being brought to school, and the general disruption to the educational environment drugs have caused for schools.

Few offenses are in greater need of strong board policy clearly stating that all violators of the school's drug policy will be dealt with not only administratively, but in each and every case in which an illegal substance is seized, the case will also be referred to the proper legal authorities. This policy *must* be uniformly enforced in *all* schools and any administrator who fails to carry out the intent of the board of education policy and the superintendent's directives must be dealt with immediately.

Many events occur in schools in which the administrator needs to have latitude in handling the event. However, drug violations are not such events. The strongest and most effective *prevention strategy* is to have a strong, well-publicized, uniformly enforced drug policy. Everyone—not only students but also parents, teachers, law enforcement officials, court officials, and the general public — must be made aware of the school's stance on drugs. Issue a simple public statement that says in effect:

The Board of Education views its responsibility for providing a safe and secure educational environment as a serious commitment to the community. Illegal drugs, including alcohol, have no place on school property. The decision to use and abuse drugs is a personal one which the Board of Education cannot make. However, let it be known that the Board of Education will do everything within its legal rights to make the use and abuse of illegal drugs a high risk occupation on school property.

It is amazing the support you will receive from both the public and the students for taking this strong stand. School districts that have enacted such a policy and whose school administrators uniformly enforce the policy have been able to show a reduction in drug violations. Many students will use the policy as a means of combating peer pressure to become involved with drug use on school property. Remember this will not stop kids from using drugs, it will only restrict their use of drugs on school property. From an administrator's point of view, keeping drugs out of school is his/her primary objective. What kids do after school and on weekends is someone else's responsibility.

RESPONSE PROCEDURES

1. When suspected drugs come into the possession of an administrator the following procedures should be followed:
   a. Place the suspected drug in a clear plastic sandwich bag.
   b. *Wash your hands* (you do not know what the drug is or what it has been treated with).
   c. Place the plastic bag in an envelope and seal the envelope.
   d. Write the date, time, from whom the suspect drug was taken on the envelope. If more than one person had custody of the drug prior to its coming into the possession of the administrator, have each person who handled the suspected drug sign the envelope. (This establishes a chain-of-custody.)
   e. Call the police to pick up the suspected drug and run a field test on the substance. A positive field test will establish sufficient probable cause to warrant administrative action. A chemist's report will be required prior to criminal trial.
   f. Have the police officer picking up the suspected drug

provide a written, signed receipt for the drug. Retain this receipt with the case file pending court action.

g. If suspected drugs cannot be picked up prior to school closing, lock the drugs in a safe, secure place. Do not, under any circumstances, decide to take the drugs home with you for safekeeping. Nothing in the law allows an administrator to transport illegal drugs on his/her person.

h. Obtain written statements from all parties involved.

i. Take appropriate *administrative action*.

2. If no drugs are recovered and a student is suspected of being under the influence of some type of substance, your response is rather limited. It is suggested that the student be treated as a "sick child," meaning the parents are called and asked to respond to the school because there is something "wrong" with his/her child. There are a number of reasons why kids sometimes act "wacko" and it may not involve drugs. Record the incident about the student; and if repeated incidents occur, you are on firmer grounds for raising the issue of possible drug involvement with the parents.

3. Plan for the reentry process of the student to school. The fact that a student has been suspended and criminally charged with a drug offense does not necessarily mean you will not have to deal with this individual at some later time. Plans should be made for the readmittance of the student. This may involve counseling, restriction of activities, loss of privileges, having a contact person assigned to the individual — one in whom the student feels he/she can confide.

INVESTIGATIVE TECHNIQUES

The most common drug problem a school administrator faces is the persistent rumor that drugs are being used on campus. Very often the information is not specific and one is left with the information that drugs are being used on the back parking lot, the bathrooms, the faculty lounge, in a stairwell, etc. The moment an administrator decides to check out the rumor, word has already reached the area he/she is planning to observe. By the time he/she gets there the action has disappeared. The following are suggestions for circumventing the "cons" communication system:

1. surveillance cameras
2. trained narcotic dog
3. restrict access to bathrooms
4. sign-in — sign-out sheets in each classroom
5. student and faculty parking lot stickers
6. police assistance
7. anonymous information center.

Remember the intent is to "make schools a high risk area for drug use and abuse." Some of these suggestions may at first shock or disturb many educators. They do sound rather clandestine in nature, but every one of them is absolutely legal and will very quickly alert the students, faculty, and parents that you mean business.

Let's explore each suggestion more fully, the rationale for using them, and the anticipated results each will provide.

Surveillance cameras. Cameras should only be used outdoors. No one is suggesting that cameras be used in bathrooms or other enclosed areas. However, for outdoor use, particularly in parking lots, athletic fields, and areas not easily observed from inside the school, a good 35mm camera with a telephoto lens is very effective. Place the photographer in a vehicle, such as a van. Using a board of education vehicle which students are accustomed to seeing can be effective. Have the photographer "shoot" the various activities that are taking place. It is amazing what you will capture on film.

After the film is developed, identify the students who appear to be engaged in illegal activity. Keep in mind that a photograph of a student passing a "bong" or marijuana pipe around is not sufficient proof that the pipe contains marijuana. No criminal action can be taken on the sole basis of the photographs. If the person being photographed, however, is holding a gun and the person it is being pointed at has his/her hands raised, you have a strong case for charging that individual with robbery.

Not so in the case of suspected drug use. The value of the picture is two-fold. First, it identifies the student or students who are probably involved in drug activity and, second, it gives you a powerful tool during a parent/student conference. And that is the real purpose of the photograph — to have something to show the parents during the conference. Every educator who has ever been involved in a student/parent conference has heard the famous words "Not my child"; "You must mean someone else." Or "My child doesn't use drugs," or "Prove it."

With a photograph you merely ask the student to explain to his/her parents what he/she was doing in the photograph. How the tone of the conference changes! You are not accusing the student of any wrongdoing and you haven't even mentioned the word drugs. All you want is the student to explain satisfactorily to the parents what was going on. Ninety-nine out of 100 times the student is speechless. No explanation will satisfy the parents. Your point has been made and the conference can proceed with everyone's attention.

Trained narcotic dogs. It has been said that dogs are man's best friend and that may be so. But what you never want to forget is that a dog is a dog is a dog. Granted they have certain abilities that most humans lack, but we humans have the ability to think and to reason, and dogs don't.

The use of narcotic dogs must be supervised closely and procedures established about how dogs will be used and under what conditions. Dogs are great for sniffing lockers, bathrooms, cars, and other similar type areas. They should *never be used to search humans.*

In a recent civil case, a female student was accused of having drugs on her person after a narcotic dog "alerted" when passing this student. After extensive questioning, which included a strip search of the female, no drugs were found. What came out in the lawsuit which followed was the fact that the female student had a female dog in heat at home. That is what the narcotic dog "alerted" to.

Dogs can be an effective psychological tool when used properly. Never lose track of the fact, however, that a human decision must still be made and the dog should only be viewed as a tool for establishing "reasonable suspicion," not conclusive evidence that drugs are present.

Limited access to bathrooms. If "johns" were used only for the purpose for which they were designed! Unfortunately, as every educator knows, bathrooms are used as the meeting place for all types of activity. A quiet place for boy to meet girl or girl to meet boy, the local gambling casino, the marketplace where goods and services are bartered and shared, and every once in a while a place where bodily functions are attended to. No one likes "potty patrol," least of all teachers and administrators. However, if that is where the action is, then administrators and teachers must also be there.

By analyzing carefully which bathrooms pose the greatest problem, a decision can be made about which bathrooms can be closed for at least part of the day. As long as several are kept open there should not be too much of an outcry that you are denying students their right to have total access to every bathroom facility in the school. By closing several bathrooms you increase your ability to monitor the ones remaining open.

Sign-in and sign-out classroom sheets. In addition to helping to control the drug problem, this strategy has many benefits. The vast majority of *all security* problems stem from the simple fact that far too many students are allowed in the halls during class time without proper authority or supervision. When this situation exists you will not only have a drug problem but you will find a large number of locker thefts, thefts of school property, trespassers, fights, assaults, robberies, and extortions.

The sign-in/sign-out procedure provides administrators with a very valuable tool for monitoring student activities. With the lists, administrators are able to identify quickly those persons who were out of their classrooms at the time an event occurred. The list will not help much the first couple of times, but by the third event you will probably find several students whose names appear on each list. You can then focus your attention on this small group rather than on the entire student body.

Parking stickers. There is no more effective way to control motor vehicle traffic at a high school than through the use of parking stickers. It makes the task of spotting *outsiders'* cars so much easier. Your custodial personnel, gym teachers, and driver education teachers can assist in identifying cars that do not belong on school property. The police can be called and furnished the tag number of an offending car.

With a tag listing of the vehicle's owner, a letter can be sent to the owner advising the person that on a certain date, at a certain time, a vehicle registered to him/her was observed on school property. The administrator can then advise the owner of the school's policy on "visitors" and request cooperation in the future.

The next time the car shows up on school property and the driver does not report to the office to register as a guest, you are able to file trespassing charges against the owner.

Many times students from other schools who cut classes visit their friends at another school. A letter to the parents is most beneficial in letting the parents know their youngster is some place where he/she shouldn't be. Also, a phone call to the student's regular school will put officials there on notice that students are skipping.

Police assistance. Educators should not try to become experts in drug identification. The police are trained and have the resources for identifying all types of drugs. It is becoming increasingly important to conduct a field test on suspected drugs if administrative action is going to be taken against a student. This is particularly true if a long term suspension (over five days) is contemplated.

Without a field test you cannot know if cigarette has been treated with PCP or some other type of drug. Nor can you tell if that green leafy substance is actually marijuana. A field test is simple and inexpensive so don't overlook its use.

In addition to handling all suspected drugs, police are most interested in receiving information about automobiles that might be involved in drug dealings. Furnish the tag numbers your staff collect as part of the parking lot surveillance to the police. You never know when that tag number will assist an ongoing investigation.

Do not expect your local police to get excited over small quantities of drugs. The availability of illegal drugs boggles the mind. Most police departments are concerned with large shipments of drugs, tons in fact; it is a little difficult for them to become excited over one or two "joints" of marijuana.

This simple fact is probably the most difficult issue for educators to understand. No one, including the police and the courts, is going to give you very much help. They have neither the manpower nor the time to devote to the school drug problem. Therefore, the suggestions offered in this section are of the "self-help" variety. With the exception of the narcotic dog, all the suggestions are designed to be implemented and carried out by school people.

Anonymous information system. Do not overlook the fact that numbers of students, teachers, and parents have or might have information about drugs in school. A system needs to be established whereby persons with information can relate it to a school official without the necessity of identifying themselves.

The most effective means of collecting this information is by phone. Perhaps a phone number could be advertised as one that a person having information about drug or any other illegal activity can call without the fear of being identified.

Granted, you cannot always take action just because a caller says someone is dealing drugs. You can, however, develop an information file and systematically collect and evaluate the information received. You never know when that little piece of information will allow you to complete a puzzle.

OTHER CONSIDERATIONS

The drug problem will be with us until such time as something else comes along that will be as appealing as drugs currently are to youth. Educators do not have the luxury of being able to ignore the problem. It is theirs to deal with and deal with it they must. The important issue to keep in mind is that educators are not alone. It is imperative that all members of the school community become involved in helping to control the problem.

Extortion

Extortion: The use of "mild" threats or intimidation to demand money or something of value from another.

Subcategories:
1. a. actual
   b. attempted
2. (1) value under $5.00
   (2) value over $5.00

Note: Extortion has become synonymous with the taking of lunch money. This act most often occurs in elementary and middle level schools. Seldom is extortion a problem in senior high school.

1. Be on the constant alert for this activity. Often the offenders do not understand the consequences of their acts. They don't understand that extortion is a crime.

2. Note particularly any changes that occur in younger students' behavior. The young person who is being victimized will show a distinct change in behavior. For example, if a child buys his/her lunch every day and then suddenly stops buying lunch and is not bringing lunch, it could be a strong indication that his/her lunch money is being taken. The cafeteria people will be the first to detect these changes and it is, therefore, important to bring this type of activity to their attention.

3. For younger students, it is a good idea to get the lunch money out of their keeping as soon as possible. Many schools have the policy that the classroom teacher collects lunch money the first thing in the morning and returns it to the youngster at the appropriate time. For middle school and junior high school students, this is not a practical solution.

4. Keep an eye on the school "bullies," both male and female. If they know their actions are being watched, they will most likely think twice before attempting to take money from fellow students.

5. Extortion may take place outside the school. Bus stops and routes taken by walking students are also "prime pickings." These areas need to be monitored on a random basis.

6. Whenever students are bringing money to school for whatever reason—field trips, school pictures, school movies, bake sales, yearbooks, class rings, athletic events, etc.—collect the money first thing in the morning. Have receipts issued with the students' names on them for admittance to events or for the purchase of items. The name is critical because if the receipt is lost or stolen, it will be useless to the finder or thief.

7. Treat extortion as a serious offense. Students, regardless of age, must learn that they will be held accountable for their actions. Just getting the property back to its rightful owner and excusing the offending student with a warning is not sufficient.

Response Procedures

1. Upon notification that an extortion has taken place, ask the victim to give a detailed account. With younger children this is a difficult task but nevertheless an important one. There may be some hesitancy on the part of the victim to come forward to admit that something of value was taken. That is why, especially with younger children, it is so important to be alert to changes in behavior.
2. Prepare an Incident Report of the event. Don't trust your memory. Besides, there may be more than one administrator to whom such events are reported. Accurate records are very important for several reasons, not the least of which is that these reports enable you to do Incident Profiling.
3. Notify the parents.
4. Notify the police.

Investigative Techniques

1. As stated earlier, watch for changes in student behavior. This will not only tip you off to possible victims, but it is just as likely to identify the extortionist. If suddenly Johnny or Mary is acting like the big spender on campus and you know that neither one has hit the state lottery, you may have an excellent indication that he/she is up to no good.
2. The experienced educator has learned how to read young people like barometers. Use these skills you have developed over the years. You won't be far off by listening to your instincts.
3. Listen to what students are saying. If extortion is going on in your school, someone will talk about it. Critical listening is extremely important.

Other Considerations

1. Whether extortions are in fact being committed or only rumored to be taking place, they are a fear-inducing event. If students believe extortion is taking place, parents will soon be aware of their concern.

2. Once fear has been introduced into your school, you will have a difficult time trying to convince people that their fears are unfounded. That is one of the reasons a proactive stance is strongly advocated in dealing with all security issues. An administrator is in a much stronger position by making a definitive statement about a certain event, based upon actual information, than by dodging the issue or flatly denying the existence of such an event when the students, parents and faculty have knowledge to the contrary.

Larceny/Theft

Larceny: The unlawful taking of property belonging to another with the intent of depriving the rightful owner access or use of the property. (Offense occurs when school is legally open.)

Note: For schools it is important to differentiate between the loss of school property that occurs when the school is closed and all employees or persons having legal use of the facility have left the premises, and the loss of school and/or personal property that occurs when the school is legally open for use.

The category of *burglary* is used to denote acts of theft that occur when the building is closed.

Subcategories:
1. a. school property
   b. personal property
   c. inventory loss
2. (1) value under $50.00
   (2) value over $50.00

PREVENTION STRATEGIES

By definition, larceny occurs when the school is open to the public. Therefore, in developing preventive strategies it is important to look at the level of adult supervision during critical time periods. The use of school buildings can be divided into five major time periods:

Period 1: From the time the first employee enters the building until school officially begins.

Period 2: Normal school day.

Period 3: After school activity time.

Period 4: Evening activity time.

Period 5: Weekend activity time.

During each of these identifiable time periods, the level of adult supervision will vary. During Period 1, there may only be a custodian and/or cafeteria workers in the school. Period 2 has the most adult supervision. Periods 3, 4, and 5 represent the time when the school is most vulnerable to larcenies because there are fewer adults in the building. If care has not been taken to properly secure property, it becomes an open invitation for someone to walk away with school and/or private property.

Unfortunately, it is not always the "outsider" we must be most concerned about. A large percentage of larcenies are committed by "insiders," i.e., students and staff. For this reason it is important not to place undue temptation before them. With this uncomfortable thought in mind, let's take a look at some preventive strategies:

1. Review the strategies listed for the prevention of property loss due to burglary. These strategies are just as effective for preventing larcenies.

2. Special consideration must be given to the handling of money. Vast amounts of money are collected on a fairly regular basis in our schools, but many people have a cavalier attitude about the handling of this money. Sponsors of various school activities collect money for field trips, school pictures, yearbooks, class rings, caps and gowns, candy sales, bake sales. The list is almost endless.

   The following suggestions are strongly recommended for the handling of money:

   a. All money should be collected as soon as possible after school opens.

   b. The money, both cash and checks, should immediately be turned in to the school secretary or bookkeeper along

37

with a list of names of those from whom the money was collected.

    c. The bookkeeper and/or secretary should issue a two-part receipt for the money. One goes to the teacher/staff person who turned in the money, and the second copy remains with the secretary/bookkeeper.

    d. All vending machines should be emptied daily of cash and the money turned in, following the same procedures with regard to receipts for cash taken.

    e. Money should never be stored in a locked or unlocked desk drawer.

    f. At the close of business every day, a bank deposit should be made.

3. Discourage students and staff from bringing expensive personal items to school.

4. Musical instruments pose unique problems for schools. Record the make, model, and serial number of all instruments, both school owned and privately owned. Keep this information in a central location.

RESPONSE PROCEDURES

1. Upon notification of stolen property, initiate a thorough search for the missing property.

2. Check sign-in and sign-out sheets to ascertain who was the last person who had responsibility for the equipment.

3. Notify the police.

4. If stolen property belonged to a student, notify the parents.

5. Make an Incident Report of the theft and check your Incident Profile records for similar events.

INVESTIGATIVE TECHNIQUES

1. Ascertain, as nearly as you can, that the theft actually occurred. Youngsters sometimes "lose" personal items and it becomes very difficult to tell mom that they lost a $400 musical instrument.

2. Adults also may have hidden reasons for reporting personal property as stolen. Don't be entirely skeptical, just cautious.

3. Try to narrow the time frame in which the property was stolen. The closer you are able to identify the time an item was stolen, the greater the opportunity to develop possible suspects.

4. Check the area from which the property was stolen. Are there any signs of forced entry into a locked desk or hall locker, etc.?

5. Determine who had access to the area or location where the theft occurred.

6. Check the working conditions of locks and lockers. Hall lockers or gym lockers can often be opened by striking the locker in a specific place.

7. Were there any unusual events or activities in the school at the time the theft occurred? Would delivery personnel or maintenance workers have had access to this affected area?

8. Put the word out that you want the property back, with no questions asked. Remember the most important factor is getting the property back to the owner, not prosecuting the thief.

9. Have custodians check trash bins for the missing property. Depending upon the size of the item stolen and the time of day the theft occurred, the thief may have had to hide the item until after school.

10. It is also a good idea to have the area surrounding the school checked. This is particularly true in the early grades. Youngsters often will take something and then not know what to do with it. The first thing that comes to mind is to hide the property. Have the gym classes walk the edge of athletic fields and any wooded area near the school. It is amazing what they will find.

OTHER CONSIDERATIONS

1. The theft of personal property cannot be ignored. People get very upset when their personal property is stolen. If a

rash of thefts occurs and students don't feel that administrators are doing anything about them, vigilante groups will form; and what started out as a property offense can quickly escalate to physical attacks.

2. Special care must be taken when outside groups use the school. Always obtain the name, address, and phone number of the person(s) in charge of the activity.

3. Insist that salespeople who are in the school selling merchandise, such as class rings, take reasonable precautions with their merchandise. It is recommended that these people be provided a room with one door and that some type of barrier, such as tables, are placed to separate the students from the items to be picked up or selected.

4. Insist that adequate supervision be provided at school dances, plays, and athletic events where money is collected for admission and that the adults take responsibility for the counting and depositing of all collected money.

Robbery

Robbery: Robbery is the use of "strong" threats, fear, or intimidation to take money or something of value which is under the direct control of another.

Subcategories:

1. a. actual
   b. attempted
2. (1) weapon used—value under $5
   (2) weapon used—value over $5
   (3) weapon used—nothing obtained
   (4) no weapon used—value under $5
   (5) no weapon used—value over $5
   (6) no weapon used—nothing obtained

PREVENTION STRATEGIES

1. The single most important strategy for preventing robberies or any criminal offense against persons rests in your ability

to create an environment that is perceived as a "high risk" area for the commission of a crime. This is not some euphemistic notion. It is accomplished by making security a high priority within the school. Through the deployment of staff and through the supervision of students, a "security presence" can be established to discourage would-be criminals. Through your example as a caring, involved, highly visible administrator, other staff members will become involved as aggressive, proactive members of your team. Students will see this level of involvement and the word will quickly travel that this school is no place to "mess around."

2. Request your local police to make periodic checks of the exterior of your school during the regular school day. Invite the officers into your school and have them walk through the halls with you. If this is done every so often, people will soon get the idea that they cannot predict when the police or other kinds of security personnel will be in the school. This can have a very stabilizing impact.

3. There are Target Hardening Techniques that can be used to limit the degree of vulnerability. They include:
   a. When money is being counted, do so in a secure area.
   b. Do not have money in view in the main office.
   c. When cafeteria personnel are counting the day's receipts, make sure the back kitchen door is locked.
   d. If possible, vary the route and the time bank deposits are made.
   e. As soon as school is over, have the building custodians secure all exterior doors.
   f. If parent conferences are scheduled with teachers after school, conduct the conferences in an area where other people are, not in the back of the school in an isolated classroom.
   g. Arrange for police and/or security to be present for evening activities at which admission is charged.
   h. As part of your normal routine, conduct "hall sweeps" during the day. A hall sweep is nothing more than having staff challenge anyone found in the hallways during class times. This is very effective for identifying outsiders who have no business in your school.

i. Pay particular attention to areas students frequent when not in class. Parking lots, bathrooms, and secluded locations around the exterior of the school are prime locations for robberies.

RESPONSE PROCEDURES

1. Robbery is a felony. It is a serious crime. Call the police. Do not attempt to handle a robbery as a disciplinary matter.
2. If the victim has been injured, obtain medical help and notify the parents.
3. Preserve the crime scene. Don't allow anyone access to the area until the police have arrived.
4. Prepare an Incident Report, noting the time you were notified and what actions you took.

INVESTIGATIVE TECHNIQUES

None—Robbery is a police matter.

OTHER CONSIDERATIONS

1. A high percentage of all robberies involving students in secondary schools are drug related. Very often the first story told is not a true rendering of the facts.
2. If the victim has been involved with drugs in the past, make sure the police are made aware of this fact.
3. Also keep your eye open for the youngster who was given money by his/her parents for a particular purpose and then used the money for some other purpose. Robbery is often claimed to explain where the money went.
4. Robbery is a fear-inducing event. You will need to be prepared for inquiries from upset parents and the media. It is important that you obtain factual information about the event and be prepared to answer questions. Steps must be taken to allay any fears other students or staff members may have as the result of a *bona fide* robbery.

Sex Offenses

Sex Offenses:

Subcategories:

1. a. actual
   b. attempted

2. (1) rape
   (2) sodomy
   (3) child molestation
   (4) indecent exposure
   (5) sexual intercourse—consenting partners
   (6) obscene phone call

PREVENTION STRATEGIES

Most sex offenses do not occur during the normal school day. They are more likely to occur either on the way to school, on the way home from school, or in the community. Although a school cannot do a great deal to prevent sex offenses, some steps can be taken to reduce the opportunity for them to occur.

1. For schools utilizing female safety patrols, it is wise to assign female students to posts that are in view of other posts. What you want to do is reduce the number of isolated posts.

2. Discussion should be held with all students involved in the safety patrol program about issues that affect their personal safety. The police can assist by locating appropriate materials to be used for these discussions. The purpose is not to frighten students but to make them more aware of their surroundings and the need to be alert to possible problem situations.

3. Faculty members should be made aware of the potential danger sex offenses pose for their students. Of great importance is the need for teachers and other staff members to know how reported sex offenses are to be handled in the event a student reports such an offense to them.

Response Procedures

Upon notification that a student has been the victim of a sex offense, do the following:

1. Call the parents.
2. Call the police.
3. Isolate the victim until the police and parents arrive.
4. Protect the crime scene, if the event occurred on school property.
5. Do not question the victim. With younger students it is extremely important for the investigating officer to hear the first story the youngster tells, not the third, fourth, or fifth version.
6. Prepare an Incident Report.

Investigative Techniques

None—All sex offenses are police matters.

Other Considerations

1. The victim of a sexual offense may not always come forth with the report. Certain staff members, such as a school nurse/aid, a secretary, or a guidance counselor may be sought out by students having problems. It is imperative that these people be particularly sensitive to changes in the behavior of students.
2. Treat every reported sex offense as a serious matter. Do not let prior knowledge of a student's promiscuous behavior influence your handling of a reported offense. Most states have statutory offenses which state that below a certain age, no female can legally give consent to sexual acts.

Trespassing

Trespassing: The unlawful presence on school property.

Subcategories:

1. a. suspended student
   b. nonstudent

2. (1) while trespassing, committed another offense
   (2) while trespassing, committed no other offense

PREVENTION STRATEGIES

1. The key to controlling trespassers is to first control the students. If a school allows excessive use of hall passes or no passes at all, it is virtually impossible to control trespassers. If on the other hand halls are clear during class periods, then the identification and subsequently the control of trespassers is simplified.

2. A good idea for controlling students and legitimate visitors in a school involves the use of two distinct types of passes. For classroom use, each teacher is issued one large 12″ × 15″ brightly colored pass with the room number written in large print. In the center of the 'pass' is a place to fasten the normal size hall pass which contains the student's name, destination, and time of issuance. All classroom passes are the same bright color—deco green, for example. All visitors passes are the same size but a different color. On this pass you may want to include a floor plan of the school showing the location of various classrooms. When administrators or teachers in the hall see someone without one of these brightly colored pass boards, they immediately know there is a trespasser in their midst.

3. For the control of parking lots, it is strongly recommended that a student/faculty parking sticker system be implemented. Again, when cars are detected on the premises that do not display a current sticker, the assumption can be made that either there is a legitimate visitor on campus or there is an outsider. The tag number can be recorded, a check made with the office to see if the tag belongs to a visitor's car and, if not, the police can be called for assistance.

4. Both of these strategies help to create a "security presence" in the school. People will quickly realize they cannot wander the school undetected.

5. Many schools, particularly high schools, use a student ID card system. For some schools it is very effective while for

others it has been less than a total success. The problem seems to arise with "forgotten" and "lost" ID cards. If you can work out that problem, then you can probably have a successful ID system. It also seems the more times a student has to use the card, the less likely he or she is to forget or lose the card.

6. Hall sweeps are effective for controlling unwanted hall activities. As discussed earlier, hall sweeps are most effective if they are performed on a random basis without prior announcement. Teachers should be advised that if any of their students are picked up in a hall sweep and the student is without the proper hall pass, they are going to be held accountable for allowing the student to be out of class.

7. Another strategy that has been used with some success is when a student is found out of class, the student is placed in the nearest classroom for the remainder of the period. It doesn't take long for the recipients of these unwanted students to let the offending teachers know exactly how they feel about having their classes disrupted by the professional hall walkers. Be prepared to act as mediator as discussions can become quite heated in the faculty lounge.

RESPONSE PROCEDURES

1. Upon notification that outsiders are in the building, assemble available staff and conduct a thorough search for the individual(s). Once they are located, offer assistance to them in case they are "lost"; and in the event they have no lawful business in the school, advise them to leave. It is not advisable to attempt to restrain an outsider if he or she wants to leave. Remember, you don't get paid for making arrests. All you want is the individual out of your building.

2. When an outsider is identified, make mental note of what the person is wearing and a general description of the person. If that individual refuses to leave or runs from you, you will have a description to give to the police.

3. After-school and evening activities present a greater problem in controlling outsiders. About the only suggestion is to

have your custodians and activity sponsors alert to the problem and summon the police if the problem persists.

INVESTIGATIVE TECHNIQUES

1. Buy yourself an inexpensive pocket camera, the kind that fits easily into a pocket. Carry it with you at all times. In the event you encounter outsiders, whip out the camera and take their picture. It is amazing to watch the change in behavior when someone thinks his or her picture has been taken. The person will become either very cooperative or run like the devil. Either way, you have accomplished your mission. The trespasser has been dealt with. P.S.—Having film in the camera is not important. This is psychological warfare at its best.

2. Some schools have had success in dealing with trespassers by using the following technique: Once the main office has been notified that an outsider is in the building, the principal or other administrator makes an announcement over the PA system that there are unwanted persons in the school and each teacher should go immediately to his/her classroom door and see if the unwanted persons are in the vicinity. When the person is confronted by three or four teachers he/she quickly departs.

OTHER CONSIDERATIONS

1. Never, never get in a hare-and-hound chase. Nothing looks more foolish than an adult chasing some fleet-footed rascal down a hallway. This is one race you can never win, so don't attempt it.

2. Serious consideration should be given to lassoing the first trespasser you apprehend and tying the individual to the flagpole for a week or two. Nothing like setting a good example for the rest of the community.

Vandalism

Vandalism: The willful and malicious destruction of property belonging to another.

Subcategories:
1. a. school property
   b. private property
2. (1) value under $50
   (2) value over $50

Note: Vandalism is a category of offense that should be used only
to reflect damage to school property. It must not be used to
classify acts of arson, burglary, larceny, or normal wear
and tear associated with building and equipment use. This
distinction is critical when programs are developed for the
prevention of vandalism. A program that is effective for
dealing with vandalism may not be effective for dealing
with arson, burglary, or larceny.

Before we discuss prevention strategies, it is important to develop an understanding of the nature of vandalism. Anyone who
has ever been involved with a school in any capacity has come to
know anger, frustration, disappointment, hostility, despair, and
even dismay when confronted with acts of vandalism. The reason
for these feelings is that most of us have a difficult time understanding why a person vandalizes. If we were able to interview
every youngster who vandalizes, we would be amazed at the
variety of reasons given for doing it. Such a list of reasons would
range from "I didn't mean to," to "because it's fun."

Richard F. Thaw, II, suggests vandalism should be viewed as a
subset of property destruction. Further, property destruction
should be viewed from three different yet interrelated dimen-
sions. He classifies these as *Hostility-Directed Acts, Acts of
Thoughtlessness,* and *Acts of Carelessness.* The examples he uses to
illustrate his point are well known to every school person.

Hostility-directed acts are those events in which the motive is to
seek revenge, change, or gain. Acts of *thoughtlessness* are events
that are motivated by a need to "play." His example is about two
boys who are returning a movie projector to audiovisual storage.
They race down the hallway with the projector on a cart and the

cart turns over, damaging the projector. The boys didn't start out with the intent to damage the projector. They just didn't think about the consequences of their act. Acts of *carelessness* are best illustrated by youngsters who litter or "trash" other students' lockers. Again there is no intent to do permanent damage. They just didn't think about the fact that someone has to clean up the mess.

Thaw also points out that these classifications are not exclusive. There is frequent overlap among them. An act that starts out as one of *thoughtlessness*, can escalate into a *hostility-directed* act, as can an act of *carelessness*. His point is that traditional approaches for controlling vandalism will work only on the hostility-directed acts and will have little or no impact in controlling acts involving thoughtlessness or carelessness. The latter two are best controlled by making kids aware of the consequences of their acts rather than attempting to use standard security approaches for controlling this type of behavior.

The authors (S. D. Vestermark and Peter Blauvelt) of *Controlling Crime in the School: A Complete Security Handbook for Administrators,* took a somewhat different approach to vandalism. Traditionally, vandalism has been viewed from only one dimension—monetary. The seriousness of an act of vandalism was determined by how much money it cost to repair/replace the damaged property. But there is another dimension to vandalism, and that is its "social cost." It is defined as the impact an act of vandalism has upon the educational program, or upon individual students, or upon "groups" of students. The following examples illustrate social costs:

Impact upon the educational program. Vandals enter a school and destroy all the school records, or they damage/destroy numerous pieces of audiovisual equipment, or they plug up sinks and flood portions of the school. Any one of these events has an adverse effect upon the school's ability to function. Not only do such acts cost a great deal of money to repair and/or replace, but often they cause the school to be closed for several days.

Impact upon individual students. Vandals enter a third grade classroom and destroy all of the holiday projects the students have been working on. They also take time to kill the pet animals the children were raising. If we viewed this event purely from a monetary point of view, we probably would not view this act of vandalism as a serious event. However, when we take into consideration the emotional impact such an event will have upon the students of the third grade class, we quickly see that this act of vandalism is indeed a serious one and steps will have to be taken to prevent similar acts from occurring.

Impact upon identifiable "groups" of students. There are times when acts of vandalism are directed at the personal property of students who are viewed as sharing certain common traits or characteristics. Every school has such groupings of students. They may be known as the "jocks," "freaks," "grits," "cowboys," "low riders," the list is almost endless. The grouping may be because certain kids ride on bus 182, or live in a certain section of town, or are of one particular race, or practice the same religion. It makes little difference how the "grouping" occurs; what is important is that when acts of vandalism are directed at the personal property of one group or another, the event can have a major impact.

By viewing vandalism from two different perspectives, *monetary* and *social*, a school administrator can reasonably judge the true seriousness of an act of vandalism and thereby make an intelligent decision on the use of limited resources to prevent such acts from recurring.

A third general way of viewing malicious vandalism has recently been developed by Bob Rubel and this writer. The system divides the social impact of malicious destruction into two subcategories: fear-inducing and non-fear-inducing. We observed, after years of study, that some acts of vandalism were directed by one group of students against another group, as previously discussed. We readily saw that these acts were potentially fear-inducing and therefore *divisive* of the educational community.

On the other hand, we also realized that some acts of vandalism were directed by many students in the school *against the school* itself, and as such were *not* fear-inducing. Actually, acts by students against the school may well be *cohesive* as they represent a graphic statement that the students do not like what is going on in the school, or do not like the teachers or administrators.

This sort of analysis—between *cohesive* and *divisive* vandalism—is vital as a planning tool, and should contribute substantially to an administrator's understanding of the social climate of his school.

Prevention Strategies

1. The key to preventing extensive acts of vandalism is the school's ability to limit access to the target, i.e., the school. Serious acts of vandalism take *time* to commit. By limiting the amount of time vandals have to commit their acts, you can significantly reduce the seriousness of an act of vandalism.

2. A properly installed, well-maintained operating burglar alarm system is the best deterrent to serious acts of vandalism. If officials are able to quickly detect illegal entries into a school, vandals will not have sufficient time to destroy audiovisual equipment, to tear a classroom apart, or to destroy office records.

3. Schools are often targeted by vandals because no one is viewed as having ownership responsibility for the property. Increasing community use of the school during nonschool hours helps to establish the idea that community members have a responsibility for the protection of the school.

4. The following is a list of antivandalism programs found to be successful in reducing vandalism. Success depends in large part on the type of community, location of the school, cooperation of the police, and the general philosophy of the powers that be about the extent to which the schools should go to reduce and/or prevent vandalism. No attempt is made here to evaluate these approaches.

   a. *Vandal Account*—School determines how much money it is willing to place in a special account. All costs for vandalism are then deducted from this account. At the end of the year any money remaining in the account is turned over to the student body for whatever they want to spend the money on. The theory is that the more money left in the account at year's end, the greater the incentive for students to stop vandalism.

   b. *Vandal Watch*—Also known as Trailer Watch. This plan calls for the placement of a house trailer on school property with the occupant of the trailer providing security functions during hours when the school is closed. This approach works best when school employees are allowed to live in the trailer. Usually, the school pays for the utilities and the employee furnishes his/her own house trailer.

c. *Community Watch*—There are a number of variations to this approach, however, the primary objective is to find ways of getting community members to watch the schools and to report to the police any suspicious activity.

d. *CB Watch*—Similar to the Community Watch except owners of CB radios are encouraged to check schools while driving around and to report all unusual or suspicious activities.

e. *Lights-out Program*—A number of schools have taken the approach that making the school as dark as possible during the night-time hours will reduce the attractiveness of the school as a target. They theorize that if vandals can't see windows breaking, then it isn't as much fun to break windows or spray paint obscenities. Some schools have found this approach not only reduces vandalism but also allows major savings in electrical costs.

Equally annoying but less costly in a monetary sense are acts of vandalism that occur when the school is open and in session. The approaches just described are only effective in controlling vandalism which occurs when school is closed, with the exception of the Vandal Account. Daytime vandalism poses a different set of requirements. Success rests primarily on the ability of the school principal to find innovative and imaginative ways of involving students in a prevention program. It is critically important that vandalism not be viewed as a "victimless" offense. You have to make vandalism a very personal event; then and only then will students, teachers, staff, and parents unite in their efforts to stop it.

RESPONSE PROCEDURES

1. Photograph all acts of vandalism. Use these photographs in your antivandalism program.

2. Report all acts of vandalism to police/security so that an investigation can be conducted. On minor acts of vandalism, make note of the time, date, and type of damage for future reference. It is not practical to report such minor acts to the police/security.

3. By using the concept of monetary and social costs, evaluate

each act of vandalism and make a determination as to what type of act was committed.

    TYPE I —High Monetary and High Social Cost
    TYPE II —High Monetary but Low Social Cost
    TYPE III—Low Monetary but High Social Cost
    TYPE IV—Low Monetary and Low Social Cost

4. As soon as possible, clean up and repair acts of vandalism. Broken windows seem to multiply if not quickly repaired. One obscene word spray painted on a wall will become 20 obscene words by the next morning.

5. Actively prosecute all vandals. Restitution should become a paramount issue. Restitution can be in the form of money or labor.

6. Don't hide the fact that the school has suffered from vandalism. The more publicity, the more irate the public, the more involved they will become.

INVESTIGATIVE TECHNIQUES

1. Vandalism is a youthful offense. Because young people who vandalize often talk about their exploits, school officials must develop good ears.

2. If vandalism is occurring during the school day and it has become a persistent problem, the following strategies should be tried:

    a. Initiate an hourly inspection of bathrooms, locker areas, and other locations where vandalism is occurring.

    b. Initiate a sign-in/sign-out log in every classroom.

    c. When vandalism is discovered, check these sheets for the names of all students who were out of class at the time the event occurred.

    d. After about the third incident you should have a list of people, several of whom appear with frequency. You now have several "suspects" to interview.

3. Initiate an Incident Profile on all acts of vandalism. This profile will identify the time, location, and target of vandals. With this information you will be able to reassign staff to cover the vulnerable spots.

4. Determine if the act of vandalism was directed at a particular

person, such as a teacher or an administrator. If you learn that the act was directed at a particular individual, find out who would want to get even or in some way retaliate against that person.

OTHER CONSIDERATIONS

1. If the act of vandalism was determined to register "high" on the social-cost scale, careful consideration must be given to offering special help to those the act most affected.
2. Determine, if possible, if the acts of vandalism are symptomatic of other more deep-seated problems in the school, such as racial tensions, labor disputes, or gang rivalries. If they are, you will need to deal with these problems before the vandalism will stop.

Weapons

Weapons: Any object that can reasonably be used to inflict bodily injury.

Subcategories:
1. a. gun
   b. knife
   c. club
   d. other
2. (1) used in the commission of a crime
   (2) not used in the commission of a crime

PREVENTION STRATEGIES

1. Let the world know that the possession and/or carrying of any type of weapon on school property will be treated as a serious offense and that any person found in violation of this school policy will be arrested and suspended from school.

2. Every morning have an administrator check with custodians and bus drivers to see if weapons have been brought to school. These people will probably know before anyone else. Special attention needs to be given to trash bins, wooded areas near parking lots, bathrooms, and any other hiding place students have discovered in the school. Bus drivers will hear youngsters talking about the presence of weapons or will see them being brought onto the bus.

3. Keep lines of communication open to students. If a weapon has been brought to school, they will talk about it and it is important to have access to students who will be willing to share this information with you.

RESPONSE PROCEDURES

1. Few words cause greater anxiety than "There's a gun in the school." Having a gun in a school or the rumor of a gun in school will ruin your day and just about wipe out any plans you had until the gun is found or the rumor is put to rest.

2. Call the police and let them know what you are confronted with and ask if they have any information about events that have occurred in the community which would lend credence to the report of a weapon in the school.

3. Alert custodial staff and have them check various "hiding places."

4. Assign staff, teachers included, to locations during lunch periods which will provide high visibility of staff. Until the weapon is found, you want to create the impression that adults are everywhere.

INVESTIGATIVE TECHNIQUES

1. Start talking. You will need to interview everyone who might have information about the weapon. Keep in mind that your primary concern is to get possession of the weapon, not to prosecute someone for possession of a weapon. Therefore, if the situation is such that you have to make some "deals" to gain possession, do so.

2. If it becomes necessary to search lockers, do it. Just be reasonable in the manner in which the search is conducted. See the section on Search and Seizure, pages 61-66.

3. If your information leads you to one suspect and that student is now being questioned, don't hesitate to do a "pat down" search of the student. This type of search involves the *external* feeling of clothing and the inspection of purses or other hand carried objects.

4. Do not, *under any circumstances,* do a "strip search." A strip search occurs when a suspect is separated from his/her clothing, and the suspect is left standing in his/her altogether, i.e., naked. If you firmly believe that your suspect has a weapon hidden on his/her body, call the parents and have them remove the student from school.

5. Try to establish why a weapon was brought to school. By establishing the possible motive for bringing the weapon(s) to school, you will have developed a logical list of suspects.

   Note: The vast majority of weapons that are brought to school are not brought with the intent to use them. Most often, weapons are brought to school for one of two reasons: for protection or for "show and tell."

OTHER CONSIDERATIONS

1. Don't deny the presence of a weapon if one in fact was recovered in the school. Answer any inquiry honestly and include in your answer what actions you took with respect to the offense.

2. Don't keep recovered weapons in the school. Call the police and turn the item(s) over to them.

Potpourri of Issues

Hostage/Terrorist/Childnapping

Few words strike greater fear or disbelief into the hearts of school administrators than the words, "They're holding children hostage!" The mere thought someone would deliberately endanger the lives of youngsters is so abhorrent to us that we have difficulty even contemplating what our response might be.

Unfortunately, this type of event is not unknown to schools. In the recent past there have been instances where schools have been targeted by terrorists. One involved terrorists in Holland who seized a school as one of two targets. Not long ago a school bus with students was seized in California and held for ransom. Incredibly, none of the children was seriously injured but the potential was there.

What is so troublesome about the potential hostage situation, as it involves schools, is that there is little anyone can do to prevent it from taking place. Schools are public places and in that lies our vulnerability. We cannot place armed guards at all entrances to our schools nor can we erect exterior barriers which would successfully prevent a terrorist's intrusion.

Reprinted with permission from Capitol Publications, Inc. Material first published in *Nation's School Report*, September 12, 1977.

Interestingly, these same restrictions hold true whether we are concerned with keeping drug dealers out of schools or stopping armed robberies in lavatories. Granted, our prevention capabilities are somewhat greater when we are dealing with students, but when we are dealing with adult terrorists we have serious problems.

Several variables affect a hostage situation: the number of hostages, the number of terrorists, the type of weapons used, the motivation of the hostage taker(s), the isolation of the school, the degree of training police agencies have had in handling hostage cases, and the preplanning school administrators have or have not done in response to a crisis situation.

Of all these variables, the only one which we as school people can control is the extent to which we have developed contingency plans for coping with emergency situations.

The following scenarios illustrate the type of situations which can occur in a school:

Situation 1: A criminal is fleeing from the police and runs into a school, grabs a student or employee, and threatens to kill them if the police do not let him go.

Situation 2: A parent comes to school and demands his/her children be brought from class and leave the school with him/her. The principal sees that the parent is acting in an irrational manner and refuses to comply with the parent's wishes. The parent produces a weapon and threatens to kill the principal or anyone else in the office if the children are not brought to him/her immediately.

Situation 3: An individual or a terrorist group specifically selects a school or several schools as suitable targets for a hostage encounter. The terrorists seize classroom(s) and demand the authorities be notified.

What makes these three situations different is the motivation which led to the event. In Situation 1 the motive is escape. The police are in pursuit and are aware the criminal is in the school. In Situation 2 the apparent motive is the release of the children. No one outside the school knows this event is taking place. In the third situation the true motives may not be known. However, the terrorists will make their demands public because it is the only way they can get to the people who can grant their demands.

There is *no guaranteed right way* to handle a hostage situation. At best, all you can do is minimize the number and severity of injuries to the hostages and protect those not directly involved. To this end, the following recommendations are made:

1. *Safety of people.* Your primary concern is for the safety of those not directly involved in the hostage situation. This means that each school will need to develop an evacuation plan whereby individuals in classrooms are quickly removed from the school. Obviously, sounding the fire alarm or making a general announcement over the public address system is *not* the way to accomplish this task. It will require an individual going to each classroom and instructing the teacher where to take her/his students. It is important that the teacher maintain control of the class and know the name of each student. Knowing the names of noninvolved students will enable you to respond to inquiries from concerned parents should the hostage situation persist over a long period of time. *All* noninvolved persons should leave the building and go to the predesignated evacuation areas.

2. *Isolating the area.* You do not want to provide the terrorists with additional hostages. The sooner a building is evacuated and the affected area isolated, the better chance the authorities will have in developing strategies for coping with the situation. The police will need to know the exact location of the hostages so that a defense perimeter can be established.

3. *Notification of authorities.* The police must be notified as soon as possible about a hostage situation. Who makes the call or from where the call is made will depend on factors unique to each situation. The important issue for whoever is making the call is the following information:
   a. number of terrorists
   b. type of weapons
   c. number of hostages
   d. number of known injuries
   e. name of adult(s) being held hostage if known
   f. type of demands being made if known
   g. any and all instructions the terrorists may have given.

If possible the caller should remain on the phone with the police so updated information may be obtained prior to the arrival of the police on the scene.

4. *Jurisdiction and responsibility for resolving hostage situation.* Once the police have been notified of a hostage situation, the primary responsibility for resolving the situation rests with the police. This does not mean that school officials will not be involved in aiding the police, but it does mean that the decision on how the situation will be handled will be made by the ranking police official on the scene. School authorities should provide whatever assistance is within their ability to furnish. The responsibility for the noninvolved students and staff will rest with the school authority on the scene. Decisions affecting noninvolved personnel and students, such as the decision to transport students home or to another school, should be made jointly by school authorities and the police.

5. *Handling of the media.* You should agree to let the police department's public information officer handle all press inquiries.

6. *Emergency Information Center.* The school system should be prepared to staff an emergency information center where parents may call for information and where calls to parents can be made.

7. *Notification of parents.* This should be one of the responsibilities of the Emergency Information Center. Staff from the affected school can be used in establishing lists of involved and noninvolved students to aid the center in making notifications. The center needs to be staffed with experienced personnel who can respond to inquiries in a calm, professional manner. The Information Center becomes more critical the longer the hostage situation continues.

It is impossible to develop a definitive plan which will meet the demands of every possible hostage situation. What is important is to have key staff members openly discuss the issues raised here. After that has been accomplished, invite your local law enforcement agency to join you in developing a better understanding of each other's role.

Search and Seizure

No issue causes more uncertainty in the minds of administrators than search and seizure. Turn to any "authority" and you will receive diverse responses to questions about your authority to conduct searches.

Fortunately, or unfortunately, you are bound by the directives and advice provided by your local legal authority. It is, therefore, inappropriate and ill-advised to discuss here the law of search and seizure and the unlimited court interpretations of these laws. Suffice it to say that school administrators have the authority to conduct "reasonable" searches of students, lockers, and vehicles when such persons and/or objects are located on school property and the administrator conducts the search pursuant to his or her official duties as a school employee.

If we assume that you have met all the criteria established by your board of education for conducting a search, some general procedures should be followed and some specific techniques should be considered.

GENERAL PROCEDURES

1. Always have a witness when conducting a search. This is for your protection as well as for strengthening testimony at the time of trial. What you don't need is to be on the witness stand and have the defense attorney ask you what happened to Johnny's $200 watch that was in his locker at the time you conducted your search. The purpose is, of course, to raise a "reasonable doubt" in the mind of just one juror that maybe Johnny did have a $200 watch and you stole it.

2. Whenever a female student is being questioned or searched, an adult female should be present. A male administrator should not leave himself open to charges or accusations of taking certain "liberties" with the female student.

3. Always conduct searches in such a manner as to reduce to a minimum any embarrassment to the person being searched.

4. When a student's locker is being searched it is always advisable to have the student present. If more than one student shares a locker, have all parties assigned to the locker pres-

ent when the locker is opened for the search. A word of caution: Having the student or students present does not mean allowing the student to open the locker or to be in close proximity to the locker. Stand the person against the opposite wall with another administrator when the locker is opened. This is for your personal safety. If the reason for the search is because you believe there is a gun in this particular locker, you don't want the student getting to it before you do.

5. Escort the student to the area where the search will be conducted. Never let the student out of yours or the escort's sight until after the search is completed. If the student is coming from a classroom, make sure all of the student's personal property is brought along. This includes books, pocketbooks, coats, jackets, hats, briefcases, lunch bags, etc. Don't allow any stops along the way. A quick visit to the bathroom, a stop to give a friend a message, or any other ruse that will distract you or the escort will in all probability result in the loss or destruction of the evidence.

6. Plan ahead when a search is anticipated. Arrange for another adult to be available to assist you. Have the room where the questioning and search is to take place selected before the student comes to you. Have the room arranged so that a straight back, armless chair is provided for the student. Tell your secretary you do not want to be interrupted while questioning and searching the student.

7. When the student is brought into your office, have him/her remove all outer garments, i.e., coats, jackets, hats, or sweaters; take possession of all objects the student is carrying; and have the student sit in the chair provided.

8. If the student has a briefcase, pocketbook, or some other personal item in which the suspected item could possibly be hidden, ask the student if he or she objects to these items being searched. If the student's response is "yes," they do object, you probably will have a legal problem if you proceed with the search. The best suggestion for handling this situation is to have someone call the parents of the student and request that they come to the school. While awaiting the arrival of the parent, keep the student under constant observation. When the parent arrives, advise him or her of the

circumstances and ask their permission to open and search the container. If the parent does not cooperate, suspend the student and have the parent remove the student from school.

Remember, your primary objective for conducting the search was to fulfill your legal duty to provide for the safety and welfare of *all* students and staff in your building, not to obtain evidence for trial.

SPECIFIC SEARCH TECHNIQUES

1. *Search of a person.* Have the individual remove all items from his or her pockets. Set these items aside until after you have completed the search of the person. Place yourself to the side of the person being searched and starting at the head work your way down the side of the body you are facing. Pay particular attention to the areas of the body where drugs, weapons, or other contraband can be hidden. A favorite trick is to wear a necklace or chain and have attached to the chain a container for drugs or even a small knife. Often the object attached to the chain will be hanging down the person's back, in the area between the shoulder blades. Another hiding place is to tape drugs or weapons to the inside of the forearm, thigh, waist, crotch, or leg calf. When you have completed one side of the individual, walk behind the person and repeat the search procedure. Take your time. It is better to be thorough than to be too quick and miss the object you are searching for.

   When you have completed the search of the individual, turn your attention to the items removed from his or her pockets. Take each item and examine it closely. Open up that pack of cigarettes and make sure the cigarettes are the only item in the package. Take the pocket lighter apart, pull the cotton wadding out of the base of the lighter, and check that area. Unscrew ballpoint pens, look inside eyeglass cases, and check the hat band and sweat band. When searching clothing, make sure you "crush" the material. Don't be satisfied with a light pat against a pocket. A small packet of drugs is not a bulky object and is easy to miss.

One common mistake, even by seasoned police officers, is to stop searching once the item being sought is found. *Don't stop searching until the person or object has been thoroughly searched.* Who's to say the individual has only one bag of marijuana or only one weapon. It's amazing what else you might find in a thorough and professional search.

2. *Search of lockers.* Start at the top shelf and remove each item from the locker. Thoroughly search each item as it is taken out and upon completion of the inspection of the object, place the object on the floor. Do not put anything back into a locker until the entire locker and its contents have been inspected.

3. *Search of vehicles.* As a general rule, anything that can be seen from outside the car can be seized and used as evidence. Again, the owner of the vehicle should be present at the time of the search. Do not go into locked glove compartments, trunks, or consoles. Employ the same technique used with the student who refused to open his or her briefcase or pocketbook. Call the parents. Driving a car to school and parking it on a school parking lot is a *privilege,* not a *right.* If the student refuses to cooperate or his/her parents refuse to cooperate, order the car from the school property and prohibit the student from bringing it back on campus.

   If you have really strong information that there is contraband of some sort locked in a vehicle, call the police and ask their advice about having them obtain a search warrant for the vehicle.

4. *Searching of other areas of the school.* No restraints are imposed for searching any part of a school you choose to search. Sections of schools that are open to the general school population are fair game. Of course, a problem will arise if something of an illegal nature is found and you then try to prove ownership of the item. Chances are that you will not be able to prove to whom the item belongs; however, your mission was successful in that the object is no longer a threat to your school.

   The question will no doubt be raised about the authority to search teacher's desks, employee lockers, or for that matter the teacher's lounge. The best advice is that so long as the item being searched is school property, you are on safe grounds. However, if you are searching an employee's locker and in this locker is a briefcase, you probably do not have legal authority to open the briefcase without the permission of the owner or without a search warrant.

POLICE ROLE IN SCHOOL SEARCHES

1. Police may conduct a search in a school when the officer who is conducting the search has a *search warrant.* You or your staff may offer whatever assistance is necessary to carry out the intent of the warrant. A search warrant will specify the place to be searched and the item(s) to be seized.
2. Police may assist you in conducting a search. The police are acting at your request. It is very logical to ask for police assistance for a number of reasons. They are better prepared to identify suspected drugs, handle weapons, and offer suggestions for carrying out your search.
3. The police *may not* legally ask you to conduct a search for them without a warrant. If you should consent to search for the police, you have at that moment become an agent for the police and are, therefore, bound by the same legal restraints as the police. It is tempting to respond to a police officer's request to go check out Johnny's locker; but you can't, and to do so places you in legal jeopardy.

HANDLING EVIDENCE

1. If your search was successful and you now have in your possession the contraband you were looking for, what do you do with it? Stick it in your bottom right hand desk drawer, give it to the assistant principal, hand it to your secretary, let it sit on the top of your desk, and go to lunch? The answer to all of the above is a resounding *no.*
2. Once evidence comes into your possession you are legally responsible for that evidence until it is turned over to the police. Protect it as if it were your most treasured personal possession.

3. Don't play with the evidence. If a gun has been confiscated, assume that it is loaded. Don't let anyone, other than the police, handle the evidence.

4. *Do not do a sniff and taste test on suspected drugs.* We have all seen "detectives" in the movies break open a package of suspected drugs and taste the contents, or hold it to their nose and take a deep whiff. It only happens in the movies. There are established field-testing techniques and the sniff-and-taste tests are not among them.

5. Place your evidence in a container, such as an envelope or box, and seal the container. Write on the sealed container the following information:
   a. description of the evidence
   b. name of the person evidence was obtained from
   c. date and time evidence came into your possession
   d. names of all persons who handled the evidence.

6. Call the police and ask them to pick up the evidence.

7. Obtain a signed receipt for the evidence from the police.

8. Prepare a written Incident Report. Make sure you include in your report what your "reasonable suspicion" was that justified your search.

9. Wash your hands. That may sound childish, but it's serious advice. You could have come in contact with PCP, LSD, coke, or any one of 100 different substances, including strychnine or rat poison. Don't take chances. Anytime you think you might have come in contact with some type of drug, wash.

These are the more important aspects of search and seizure as they pertain to schools. Books, however, have been written on the subject and, of course, cover the topic more completely. What is presented here are good practical techniques and sound advice.

Reference Materials

REFERENCE MATERIALS

S. D. Vestermark and P. Blauvelt, *Controlling Crime in the School: A Complete Security Handbook for Administrators* (New York: Prentice-Hall, 1978). Available through IRC Publications, P.O. Box 730, College Park, Md. 20740.

R. Rubel, *The Unruly School* (Lexington, Mass.: Lexington Books, 1977).

K. Baker and R. Rubel, *Violence and Crime in the Schools* (Lexington, Mass.: Lexington Books, 1980).

BIBLIOGRAPHY

Berger, M. *Violence in the Schools: Causes and Remedies.* Bloomington, Ind.: The Phi Delta Kappa Educational Foundation, 1974.
Bloch, A. M. "The Battered Teacher." *Today's Education*, March-April 1977.
————. "Combat Neurosis in Inner-city Schools." *American Journal of Psychiatry* 135 (1978): 1189–92.
Cardinelli, C. F. "Relationships of Interaction of Selected Personality Characteristics of School Principal and Custodian with Sociological Variables to School Vandalism." Doctoral dissertation, Michigan State University, 1969.
————. "Let's Get at the Causes of Youthful Vandalism." *American School Board Journal* 1 (1961): 68–69.
Clement, S. L. "School Vandalism—Causes and Cures." *NASSP Bulletin* 59 (1975): 17–21.
Cohen, S. "Property Destruction: Motives and Meanings." In *Vandalism,* edited by C. Ward. London: Architectural Press, 1973.

Cops In, Robbers Out. *Nation's Schools and Colleges,* June 1975, pp. 12–14.

Elliott, D. S. and Voss, H. L. *Delinquency and Dropout.* Lexington, Mass.: Lexington Books, 1974.

Ertukel, D. "School Security: A Student Point of View." *NASSP Bulletin* 58 (1974): 44–49.

Goldmeier, H. "Vandalism: The Effects of Unmanageable Confrontations." *Adolescence* 9 (1974): 49–56.

Juillerat, E. E., Jr. "For Worried School Districts: Here's Lots of Sensible Advice for Lasting Ways to Cut Down on School Vandalism." *American School Board Journal,* January 1974: pp. 64–69.

Madison, A. *Vandalism: The Not-So-Senseless Crime.* New York: Seabury Press, 1970.

Marvin, M.; McCann, R.; Connolly, S.; Temkin, S.; and Henning, P. *Planning Assistance Programs to Reduce School Violence.* Philadelphia: Research for Better Schools, Inc., 1976.

McGuire, W. "Violence in the Schools." *NEA Reporter,* February 1976, p. 3.

McPartland, J. M. and McDill, E. L. "Research on Crime in Schools." In *Violence in Schools: Perspectives, Programs, and Positions,* edited by J. M. McPartland and E. L. McDill. Lexington, Mass.: D.C. Heath, 1977.

Radar, H. "The Child as Terrorist: Seven Cases." *School Review,* November 1975, p. 31.

Richards, P. "Patterns of Middle Class Vandalism: A Case Study of Suburban Adolescence." Doctoral dissertation, Northwestern University, 1976.

Rubel, R. J. *The Unruly School.* Lexington, Mass.: Lexington Books, 1977.

Schwartz, S. "A New Way to Fight School Vandalism." *American School and University,* June 1973, pp. 54–55.

Stanford Research Institute. *Program for the Prevention and Control of School Vandalism and Related Burglaries.* Final Report. Menlo Park, Calif., June, 1975.

Thaw, R. F. "An Acts Against Property Model: A Case Study. An Extension of the Traditional Vandalism Model." Doctoral dissertation, United States International University (San Diego), 1976.

"Violence in the Schools: Everybody Has Solutions." *American School Board Journal,* January 1975, pp. 27–37.

Wenk, E. "Schools and the Community: A Model for Participatory Problem Solving." In *Delinquency Prevention and the Schools: Emerging Perspectives,* edited by E. Wenk. Beverly Hills, Calif.: Sage Publications, 1976.